BOOKS BY
WALTER LIPPMANN

★

A PREFACE TO POLITICS, *1913*
DRIFT AND MASTERY, *1914*
THE STAKES OF DIPLOMACY, *1915*
THE POLITICAL SCENE, *1919*
LIBERTY AND THE NEWS, *1920*
PUBLIC OPINION, *1922*
THE PHANTOM PUBLIC, *1925*
MEN OF DESTINY, *1927*
AMERICAN INQUISITORS, *1928*
A PREFACE TO MORALS, *1929*
INTERPRETATIONS 1931–1932, *1932*
INTERPRETATIONS 1933–1935, *1936*
THE METHOD OF FREEDOM, *1934*
THE NEW IMPERATIVE, *1935*
THE GOOD SOCIETY, *1937*
U.S. FOREIGN POLICY, Shield of the Republic, *1943*
U.S. WAR AIMS, *1944*
THE COLD WAR, A Study in U. S. Foreign Policy, *1947*

WITH WILLIAM O. SCROGGS

THE UNITED STATES IN WORLD AFFAIRS 1931, *1932*
THE UNITED STATES IN WORLD AFFAIRS 1932, *1933*

THE COLD WAR

THE COLD WAR:

A Study in U. S. Foreign Policy

BY WALTER LIPPMANN

NEW YORK   LONDON

HARPER & BROTHERS PUBLISHERS

11-7

THE COLD WAR

K-W

Publisher's Note

The author hoped that the book would contain the article by "X," which is referred to in the text, on "The Sources of Soviet Conduct" which appeared in the July issue of *Foreign Affairs*. We regret to state that it was not possible to obtain permission to use this article, which is printed in *The Foreign Affairs Reader*, a book just published. However, Mr. Lippmann's references to the points made by "X" are so clear that the reader of this book should have no difficulty in following the argument.

The material in this book appeared as a series
of articles in the *New York Herald Tribune*.

THE COLD WAR

INTRODUCTION

An anonymous article on "The Sources of Soviet Conduct" appeared in the quarterly journal *Foreign Affairs* for July 1947 and shortly afterwards it was republished by *Life* magazine. By its quality alone it would have commanded wide attention. For it was manifestly the work of a man who had observed the Soviet regime closely with a trained eye and an educated mind, and had arrived at a theory as to why the conduct of the Soviet government reflects "no abstract love of peace and stability, no real faith in the possibility of a permanent happy co-existence of the socialist and capitalist worlds, but rather a continuous, persistent pressure towards the disruption and weakening of all rival influence and rival power."

Almost immediately several of the leading correspondents in Washington identified the author, who signed himself "X," as being Mr. George F. Kennan who, after a tour of duty at the Embassy in Moscow, had recently been appointed by Secretary Marshall to be the Director of the Policy Planning Staff of the Department of State. The attribution was not denied. After that Mr. X's article was no longer just one more report on the Soviet regime and what to do about it. It was an event, announcing that the Department of State had made up its mind,[1] and was prepared to disclose to the American people, to the world at large, and of course also to the Kremlin the estimates, the calculations, and the conclusions on which the Department was basing its plans.

Mr. X's article is, therefore, not only an analytical interpre-

[1] At least as of March 15 approximately.

9

tation of the sources of Soviet conduct. It is also a document of primary importance on the sources of American foreign policy—of at least that part of it which is known as the Truman Doctrine.

As such I am venturing to examine it critically in this essay. My criticism, I hasten to say at once, does not arise from any belief or hope that our conflict with the Soviet government is imaginary or that it can be avoided, or ignored, or easily disposed of. I agree entirely with Mr. X that the Soviet pressure cannot "be charmed or talked out of existence." I agree entirely that the Soviet power will expand unless it is prevented from expanding because it is confronted with power, primarily American power, that it must respect. But I believe, and shall argue, that the strategical conception and plan which Mr. X recommends is fundamentally unsound, and that it cannot be made to work, and that the attempt to make it work will cause us to squander our substance and our prestige.

1.

We must begin with the disturbing fact, which anyone who will reread the article can verify for himself, that Mr. X's conclusions depend upon the optimistic prediction that the "Soviet power . . . bears within itself the seeds of its own decay, and that the sprouting of these seeds is well advanced"; that if "anything were ever to occur to disrupt the unity and the efficacy of the Party as a political instrument, Soviet Russia might be changed overnight (sic) from one of the strongest to one of the weakest and most pitiable of national societies"; and "that Soviet society may well (sic) contain deficiencies which will eventually weaken its own total potential."

Of this optimistic prediction Mr. X himself says that it "cannot be proved. And it cannot be disproved." Nevertheless, he concludes that the United States should construct its policy on the assumption that the Soviet power is inherently weak and impermanent, and that this unproved assumption warrants our entering "with reasonable confidence upon a policy of firm containment, designed to confront the Russians with unalterable counterforce at every point where they show signs of encroaching upon the interests of a peaceful and a stable world."

I do not find much ground for reasonable confidence in a policy which can be successful only if the most optimistic prediction should prove to be true. Surely a sound policy must be addressed to the worst and hardest that may be judged to be probable, and not to the best and easiest that may be possible.

As a matter of fact, Mr. X himself betrays a marked lack of confidence in his own diagnosis. For no sooner had he finished describing the policy of firm containment with unalterable counterforce at every point where the Russians show signs of encroaching, when he felt he must defend his conclusions against the criticism, one might almost say the wisecrack, that this is a policy of "holding the line and hoping for the best." His defense is to say that while he is proposing a policy of holding the line and hoping for the best, "in actuality the possibilities for American policy are by no means limited to holding the line and hoping for the best." The additional possibilities are not, however, within the scope of the authority of the Department of State: "the aims of Russian communism must appear sterile and quixotic, the hopes and enthusiasms of Moscow's supporters must wane, and added strain must be imposed on the Kremlin's foreign policies" if "the United States can create among the peoples of the world generally the impression of a country which knows what it wants, which is coping successfully with the problems of its internal life and with the responsibilities of a world power, and which has a spiritual vitality capable of holding its own among the major ideological currents of the time."

This surely is a case of bolstering up the wishful thinking of "hoping for the best"—namely, the collapse of the Soviet power—by an extra strong dose of wishful thinking about the United States. There must be something deeply defective in Mr. X's estimates and calculations. For on his own showing, the policy cannot be made to work unless there are miracles and we get all the breaks.

In Mr. X's estimates there are no reserves for a rainy day. There is no margin of safety for bad luck, bad management, error and the unforeseen. He asks us to assume that the Soviet power is already decaying. He exhorts us to believe that our own highest hopes for ourselves will soon have been realized. Yet the policy he recommends is designed to deal effectively with the Soviet Union "as a rival, not a partner, in the political arena." Do we dare to assume, as we enter the arena and get set to run the race, that the Soviet Union will break its leg while the United States grows a pair of wings to speed it on its way?

Mr. X concludes his article on Soviet conduct and American policy by saying that "the thoughtful observer of Russian-American relations will . . . experience a certain gratitude to a Providence which, by providing the American people with this implacable challenge, has made their entire security as a nation dependent upon their pulling themselves together and accepting the responsibilities of moral and political leadership that history plainly intended them to bear." Perhaps. It may be that Mr. X has read the mind of Providence and that he knows what history plainly intended. But it is asking a good deal that the American people should stake their "entire security as a nation" upon a theory which, as he himself says, cannot be proved and cannot be disproved.

Surely it is by no means proved that the way to lead mankind is to spend the next ten or fifteen years, as Mr. X proposes we should, in reacting at "a series of constantly shifting geographical and political points, corresponding to the shifts and maneuvers of Soviet policy." For if history has indeed intended us to bear the responsibility of leadership, then it is not leadership to adapt ourselves to the shifts and maneuvers of Soviet policy at a series of constantly shifting geographical and political points. For that would mean for ten or fifteen, years Moscow, not Washington, would define the issues, would make the challenges, would select the ground where the conflict was to be waged, and would choose the weapons. And the best that Mr. X can say for his own proposal is that if for a long period of time we can prevent the Soviet power from winning, the Soviet power will eventually perish or "mellow" because it has been "frustrated."

This is a dismal conclusion. Mr. X has, I believe, become bogged down in it because as he thought more and more about the conduct of the Soviet, he remembered less and less about the conduct of the other nations of the world. For while it may be true that the Soviet power would perish of frustration, if it were contained for ten or fifteen years, this conclusion is only half baked until he has answered the crucial question which remains: can the western world operate a policy of containment? Mr. X not only does not answer this question. He begs it, saying that it will be very discouraging to the Soviets, if the western world finds the strength and resourcefulness to contain the Soviet power over a period of ten or fifteen years.

2.

Now the strength of the western world is great, and we may assume that its resourcefulness is considerable. Nevertheless, there are weighty reasons for thinking that the kind of strength we have and the kind of resourcefulness we are capable of showing are peculiarly unsuited to operating a policy of containment.

How, for example, under the Constitution of the United States is Mr. X going to work out an arrangement by which the Department of State has the money and the military power always available in sufficient amounts to apply "counterforce" at constantly shifting points all over the world? Is he going to ask Congress for a blank check on the Treasury and for a blank authorization to use the armed forces? Not if the American constitutional system is to be maintained. Or is he going to ask for an appropriation and for authority each time the Russians "show signs of encroaching upon the interests of a peaceful and stable world"? If that is his plan for dealing with the maneuvers of a dictatorship, he is going to arrive at the points of encroachment with too little and he is going to arrive too late. The Russians, if they intend to encroach, will have encroached while Congress is getting ready to hold hearings.

A policy of shifts and maneuvers may be suited to the Soviet system of government, which, as Mr. X tells us, is animated by patient persistence. It is not suited to the American system of government.

It is even more unsuited to the American economy which is unregimented and uncontrolled, and therefore cannot be administered according to a plan. Yet a policy of containment cannot be operated unless the Department of State can plan and direct exports and imports. For the policy demands that American goods be delivered or withheld at "constantly shifting geographical and political points corresponding to the shifts and maneuvers of Soviet policy."

Thus Mr. X and the planners of policy in the State Department, and not supply and demand in the world market, must determine continually what portion of the commodities produced here may be sold in the United States, what portion is to be set aside for export, and then sold, lent, or given to this foreign country rather than to that one. The Department of State must be able to allocate the products of American industry and agriculture, to ration the goods allocated for export among the nations which are to contain the Soviet Union, and to discriminate among them, judging correctly and quickly how much each nation must be given, how much each nation can safely be squeezed, so that all shall be held in line to hold the line against the Russians.

If then the Kremlin's challenge to American society is to be met by the policy which Mr. X proposes, we are committed to a contest, for ten or fifteen years, with the Soviet system which is planned and directed from Moscow. Mr. X is surely mistaken, it seems to me, if he thinks that a free and undirected economy like our own can be used by the diplomatic planners to wage a diplomatic war against a planned economy at a series of constantly shifting geographical and political points. He is proposing to meet the Soviet challenge on the ground which is most favorable to the Soviets, and with the very instruments, procedures, and weapons in which they have a manifest superiority.

3.

I FIND it hard to understand how Mr. X could have recommended such a strategic monstrosity. For he tells us, no doubt truly, that the Soviet power "cannot be easily defeated or discouraged by a single victory on the part of its opponents," and that "the patient persistence by which it is animated" means that it cannot be "effectively countered" by "sporadic acts." Yet his own policy calls for a series of sporadic acts: the United States is to apply "counterforce" where the Russians encroach and when they encroach.

On his own testimony no single victory will easily defeat or discourage the patient persistence of the Kremlin. Yet Mr. X says that the United States should aim to win a series of victories which will cause the Russians to "yield on individual sectors of the diplomatic front." And then what? When the United States has forced the Kremlin to "face frustration indefinitely" there will "eventually" come "either the breakup or the gradual mellowing of the Soviet power."

There is, however, no rational ground for confidence that the United States could muster "unalterable counterforce" at all the individual sectors. The Eurasian continent is a big place, and the military power of the United States, though it is very great, has certain limitations which must be borne in mind if it is to be used effectively. We live on an island

continent. We are separated from the theaters of conflict by
the great oceans. We have a relatively small population, of
which the greater proportion must in time of war be employed
in producing, transporting and servicing the complex weapons
and engines which constitute our military power. The United
States has, as compared with the Russians, no adequate reserves of infantry. Our navy commands the oceans and we
possess the major offensive weapons of war. But on the
ground in the interior of the Eurasian continent, as we are
learning in the Greek mountains, there may be many "individual sectors" where only infantry can be used as the
"counterforce."

These considerations must determine American strategy in
war and, therefore, also in diplomacy, whenever the task of
diplomacy is to deal with a conflict and a contest of power.
The planner of American diplomatic policy must use the
kind of power we do have, not the kind we do not have. He
must use that kind of power where it can be used. He must
avoid engagements in those "individual sectors of the diplomatic front" where our opponents can use the weapons in
which they have superiority. But the policy of firm containment as defined by Mr. X ignores these tactical considerations.
It makes no distinction among sectors. It commits the United
States to confront the Russians with counterforce "at every
point" along the line, instead of at those points which we
have selected because, there at those points, our kind of sea
and air power can best be exerted.

American military power is peculiarly unsuited to a policy
of containment which has to be enforced persistently and
patiently for an indefinite period of time. If the Soviet Union
were an island like Japan, such a policy could be enforced
by American sea and air power. The United States could,

without great difficulty, impose a blockade. But the Soviet Union has to be contained on land, and "holding the line" is therefore a form of trench warfare.

Yet the genius of American military power does not lie in holding positions indefinitely. That requires a massive patience by great hordes of docile people. American military power is distinguished by its mobility, its speed, its range and its offensive striking force. It is, therefore, not an efficient instrument for a diplomatic policy of containment. It can only be the instrument of a policy which has as its objective a decision and a settlement. It can and should be used to redress the balance of power which has been upset by the war. But it is not designed for, or adapted to, a strategy of containing, waiting, countering, blocking, with no more specific objective than the eventual "frustration" of the opponent.

The Americans would themselves probably be frustrated by Mr. X's policy long before the Russians were.

4.

THE policy of containment, which Mr. X recommends, demands the employment of American economic, political, and in the last analysis, American military power at "sectors" in the interior of Europe and Asia. This requires, as I have pointed out, ground forces, that is to say reserves of infantry, which we do not possess.

The United States cannot by its own military power contain the expansive pressure of the Russians "at every point where they show signs of encroaching." The United States cannot have ready "unalterable counterforce" consisting of American troops. Therefore, the counterforces which Mr. X requires have to be composed of Chinese, Afghans, Iranians, Turks, Kurds, Arabs, Greeks, Italians, Austrians, of anti-Soviet Poles, Czechoslovaks, Bulgars, Yugoslavs, Albanians, Hungarians, Finns and Germans.

The policy can be implemented only by recruiting, subsidizing and supporting a heterogeneous array of satellites, clients, dependents and puppets. The instrument of the policy of containment is therefore a coalition of disorganized, disunited, feeble or disorderly nations, tribes and factions around the perimeter of the Soviet Union.

To organize a coalition among powerful modern states is, even in time of war and under dire necessity, an enormously difficult thing to do well. To organize a coalition of disunited, feeble and immature states, and to hold it together for a prolonged diplomatic siege, which might last for ten or fifteen years, is, I submit, impossibly difficult.

It would require, however much the real name for it were disavowed, continual and complicated intervention by the United States in the affairs of all the members of the coalition which we were proposing to organize, to protect, to lead and to use. Our diplomatic agents abroad would have to have an almost unerring capacity to judge correctly and quickly which men and which parties were reliable containers. Here at home Congress and the people would have to stand ready to back their judgments as to who should be nominated, who should be subsidized, who should be whitewashed, who should be seen through rose-colored spectacles, who should be made our clients and our allies.

Mr. X offers us the prospect of maintaining such a coalition indefinitely until—eventually—the Soviet power breaks up or mellows because it has been frustrated. It is not a good prospect. Even if we assume, which we ought not, that our diplomatic agents will know how to intervene shrewdly and skillfully all over Asia, the Middle East, and Europe, and even if we assume, which the Department of State cannot, that the American people will back them with a drawing account of blank checks both in money and in military power, still it is not a good prospect. For we must not forget that the Soviet Union, against which this coalition will be directed, will resist and react.

In the complicated contest over this great heterogeneous array of unstable states, the odds are heavily in favor of the Soviets. For if we are to succeed, we must organize our satellites as unified, orderly and reasonably contented nations. The Russians can defeat us by disorganizing states that are already disorganized, by disuniting peoples that are torn with civil strife, and by inciting their discontent which is already very great.

. As a matter of fact this borderland in Europe and Asia around the perimeter of the Soviet Union is not a place where Mr. X's "unassailable barriers" can be erected. Satellite states and puppet governments are not good material out of which to construct unassailable barriers. A diplomatic war conducted as this policy demands, that is to say conducted indirectly, means that we must stake our own security and the peace of the world upon satellites, puppets, clients, agents about whom we can know very little. Frequently they will act for their own reasons, and on their own judgments, presenting us with accomplished facts that we did not intend, and with crises for which we are unready. The "unassailable barriers" will present us with an unending series of insoluble dilemmas. We shall have either to disown our puppets, which would be tantamount to appeasement and defeat and the loss of face, or must support them at an incalculable cost on an unintended, unforeseen and perhaps undesirable issue.

5.

THERE is still greater disadvantage in a policy which seeks to "contain" the Soviet Union by attempting to make "unassailable barriers" out of the surrounding border states. They are admittedly weak. Now a weak ally is not an asset. It is a liability. It requires the diversion of power, money, and prestige to support it and to maintain it. These weak states are vulnerable. Yet the effort to defend them brings us no nearer to a decision or to a settlement of the main conflict. Worst of all, the effort to develop such an unnatural alliance of backward states must alienate the natural allies of the United States.

The natural allies of the United States are the nations of the Atlantic community: that is to say, the nations of western Europe and of the Americas. The Atlantic Ocean and the Mediterranean Sea, which is an arm of the Atlantic Ocean, unite them in a common strategic, economic and cultural system. The chief components of the Atlantic community are the British Commonwealth of nations, the Latin states on both sides of the Atlantic, the Low Countries and Switzerland, Scandinavia and the United States.

The boundaries of the Atlantic community are not sharp and distinct, particularly in the case of the Germans and the western Slavs and the dependencies and the colonies of western

Europe. But the nucleus of the Atlantic community is distinct and unmistakable, and among the nations that are indisputably members of the Atlantic community there exists a vital connection founded upon their military and political geography, the common traditions of western Christendom, and their economic, political, legal, and moral institutions which, with all their variations and differences, have a common origin and have been shaped by much the same historic experience.

Now the policy of containment, as described by Mr. X, is an attempt to organize an anti-Soviet alliance composed in the first instance of peoples that are either on the shadowy extremity of the Atlantic community, or are altogether outside it. The active proponents of the policy have been concerned immediately with the anti-Soviet parties and factions of eastern Europe, with the Greeks, the Turks, the Iranians, the Arabs and Afghans, and with the Chinese Nationalists.

Instead of concentrating their attention and their efforts upon our old allies of the Atlantic community, the makers and the shapers of the policy of containment have for more than a year been reaching out for new allies on the perimeter of the Soviet Union. This new coalition, as we can see only too clearly in Greece, in Iran, in the Arab states and in China, cannot in fact be made to coalesce. Instead of becoming an unassailable barrier against the Soviet power, this borderland is a seething stew of civil strife.

We have not succeeded in organizing the new and alien coalition of the Russian perimeter, and we have failed to consolidate, as the mounting crisis of western Europe and of Latin America shows, the old and familiar coalition of the Atlantic community. The supporters of the Truman Doctrine attribute the divisions and the paralysis of western Europe to the machinations of the Soviet Union, to its obstruction in the United Nations and in all the various peace conferences, to the propaganda, the infiltration of the communist parties. Perhaps. But their argument, if true, destroys the last reason for thinking that the policy of containment can be made to work successfully.

For the nations of the Atlantic community are not occupied by the Red Army. They cannot be occupied by the Red Army unless the Kremlin is prepared to face a full scale world war, atomic bombs and all the rest. Though impoverished and weakened, the nations of the Atlantic community are incomparably stronger, richer, more united and politically more democratic and mature than any of the nations of the Russian perimeter.

If the Soviet Union is, nevertheless, able to paralyze and disorganize them, then surely it can much more readily paralyze and disorganize the nations of the perimeter. They are already paralyzed and disorganized. They have never, in fact, been organized and effective modern states. Yet we are asked to believe that we can organize the perimeter of Russia, though the Russians are so strong and so cunning that we cannot consolidate the Atlantic community.

By concentrating our efforts on a diplomatic war in the borderlands of the Soviet Union, we have neglected—because we do not have unlimited power, resources, influence, and diplomatic brain power—the vital interests of our natural allies in western Europe, notably in reconstructing their economic life and in promoting a German settlement on which they can agree.

The failure of our diplomatic campaign in the borderlands, on which we have staked so much too much, has conjured up the specter of a Third World War. The threat of a Russian-American war, arising out of the conflict in the borderlands, is dissolving the natural alliance of the Atlantic community. For the British, the French, and all the other Europeans see that they are placed between the hammer and the anvil. They realize, even if we do not realize it, that the policy of containment, in the hope that the Soviet power will collapse by frustration, cannot be enforced and cannot be administered successfully, and that it must fail. Either Russia will burst through the barriers which are supposed to contain her, and all of Europe will be at her mercy, or, at some point and at some time, the diplomatic war will become a full scale shooting war. In either event Europe is lost. Either Europe falls under the domination of Russia, or Europe becomes the battlefield of a Russian-American war.

Because the policy of containment offers these intolerable alternatives to our old allies, the real aim of every European nation, including Great Britain, is to extricate itself from the Russian-American conflict. While we have been devoting our energies to lining up and bolstering up the Chinese Nationalists, the Iranians, the Turks, the Greek monarchists and conservatives, the anti-Soviet Hungarians, Rumanians, Poles, the natural alignment of the British, French, Belgians, Dutch, Swiss and Scandinavians has been weakened.

And so in any prudent estimate of our world position, they are no longer to be counted upon as firm members of a coalition led by the United States against the Soviet Union. We must not deceive ourselves by supposing that we stand at the head of a worldwide coalition of democratic states in our conflict with the Soviet Union.

The aim of the leading democratic states of Europe and probably also of the Americas is at best to hold the balance of power between Russia and America, and thus to become mediators of that conflict. At worst, their aim is to isolate themselves in some kind of neutrality which will spare them the dual catastrophe of being overrun by the Red Army and bombed by the American air forces.

For they cannot have reasonable confidence in what Mr. X says is sufficient ground for reasonable confidence. They cannot rely on his wishful prediction which "cannot be proved" and "cannot be disproved," that the Soviet power will break up or "mellow" when it has been frustrated for ten or fifteen years by unassailable barriers in such inaccessible "individual sectors" as Manchuria, Mongolia, north China, Afghanistan, Iran, Hungary and Rumania.

They remember Mr. Chamberlain's efforts to contain Hitler by a guarantee to Poland. They remember Mr. Hull's effort to contain Japan in China. They know that a policy of containment does not contain, that measures of "counterforce" are doomed to be too late and too little, that a policy of holding the line and hoping for the best means the surrender of the strategic initiative, the dispersion of our forces without prospect of a decision and a settlement, and in the end a war which, once begun, it would be most difficult to conclude.

6.

IT WILL be evident, I am sure, to the reader who has followed the argument to this point that my criticism of the policy of containment, or the so-called Truman Doctrine, does not spring from any hope or belief that the Soviet pressure to expand can be "charmed or talked out of existence." I agree entirely with Mr. X that we must make up our minds that the Soviet power is not amenable to our arguments, but only "to contrary force" that "is felt to be too strong, and thus more rational in the logic and rhetoric of power."

My objection, then, to the policy of containment is not that it seeks to confront the Soviet power with American power, but that the policy is misconceived, and must result in a misuse of American power. For as I have sought to show, it commits this country to a struggle which has for its objective nothing more substantial than the hope that in ten or fifteen years the Soviet power will, as the result of long frustration, "break up" or "mellow." In this prolonged struggle the role of the United States is, according to Mr. X, to react "at a series of constantly shifting geographical and political points" to the encroachments of the Soviet power.

The policy, therefore, concedes to the Kremlin the strategical initiative as to when, where and under what local circumstances the issue is to be joined. It compels the United States to meet the Soviet pressure at these shifting geographical and political points by using satellite states, puppet governments and agents which have been subsidized and supported, though their effectiveness is meager and their reliability uncertain. By forcing us to expend our energies and our substance upon these dubious and unnatural allies on the perimeter of the Soviet Union, the effect of the policy is to neglect our natural allies in the Atlantic community, and to alienate them.

They are alienated also by the fact that they do not wish to become, like the nations of the perimeter, the clients of the United States in whose affairs we intervene, asking as the price of our support that they take the directives of their own policy from Washington. They are alienated above all by the prospect of war, which could break out by design or accident, by miscalculation or provocation, if at any of these constantly shifting geographical and political points the Russians or Americans became so deeply engaged that no retreat or compromise was possible. In this war their lands would be the battlefield. Their peoples would be divided by civil conflict. Their cities and their fields would be the bases and the bridgeheads in a total war which, because it would merge into a general civil war, would be as indecisive as it was savage.

We may now ask why the official diagnosis of Soviet conduct, as disclosed by Mr. X's article, has led to such an unworkable policy for dealing with Russia. It is, I believe, because Mr. X has neglected even to mention the fact that the Soviet Union is the successor of the Russian Empire and that Stalin is not only the heir of Marx and of Lenin but of Peter the Great, and the Czars of all the Russias.

For reasons which I do not understand, Mr. X decided not to consider the men in the Kremlin as the rulers of the Russian State and Empire, and has limited his analysis to the inter-action of "two forces": "the ideology inherited by the present

Soviet leaders from the movement in which they had their political origin" and the "circumstances of the power which they have now exercised for nearly three decades in Russia."

Thus he dwells on the indubitable fact that they believe in the Marxian ideology and that "they have continued to be predominantly absorbed with the struggle to secure and make absolute the power which they seized in November 1917." But with these two observations alone he cannot, and does not, explain the conduct of the Soviet government in this postwar era—that is to say its aims and claims to territory and to the sphere of influence which it dominates. The Soviet government has been run by Marxian revolutionists for thirty years; what has to be explained by a planner of American foreign policy is why in 1945 the Soviet government expanded its frontiers and its orbit, and what was the plan and pattern of its expansion. That can be done only by remembering that the Soviet government is a Russian government and that this Russian government has emerged victorious over Germany and Japan.

Having omitted from his analysis the fact that we are dealing with a victorious Russia—having become exclusively preoccupied with the Marxian ideology, and with the communist revolution—it is no wonder that the outcome of Mr. X's analysis is nothing more definite, concrete and practical than that the Soviets will encroach and expand "at a series of constantly shifting geographical and political points." Mr. X's picture of the Soviet conduct has no pattern. It is amorphous. That is why his conclusions about how we should deal with the Soviets have no pattern, and are also amorphous.

By contrast with Mr. X, it may be useful to call in another expert, a distinguished political geographer, Professor Robert Strausz-Hupe of the University of Pennsylvania, whose article on "The Western Frontiers of Russia" appeared in the July issue of *The Review of Politics,* quarterly published by the University of Notre Dame:

"The mosaic of treaties and agreements, which forms the legal basis of Russian territorial acquisitions, is composed of strangely assorted pieces. Its general, although somewhat crude, shape was first revealed by the Soviet-German Secret Protocol of August 23, 1939. This document allocated Estonia and Latvia to the Soviet Union and established the demarcation line of the German-Soviet occupation of Poland. The Additional Protocol of September 28 transferred Lithuania to the Soviet orbit and expressed German agreement to the cession by Rumania of Bessarabia to the U.S.S.R. The latter transaction was consummated in the Soviet-Rumanian Agreement of June 28, 1940. The Soviet-Polish Treaty of August 1945 confirms, except for minor deviations, the arrangements agreed upon in the two Soviet-German Protocols. The Rumanian Peace Treaty of 1947 expressly reaffirms the validity of the Soviet-Rumanian Agreement of 1940. The parties to these transactions represent the most diverse ideologies and allegiances, none of which the Soviet Union permitted to interfere with its pursuit of strategic objectives. Where its frontiers were concerned the Soviet Union managed to overlook the distinction between friend and foe, fascism and democracy, Slav and non-Slav."

"Considered as a whole, this strange patchwork of title deeds, bound together by the military might of the Soviet Union, annuls the defeat of 1917. It restores Russia to the geographical positions held by the last Romanovs. The Baltic Republics and Bessarabia reverted—as, writing nearly twenty years ago, Isaiah Bowman predicted—to Russian domination; the territorial clauses of the Peace Treaty with Finland, outright cession of the Karelian Isthmus and Petsamo Province, and lease of a naval base at Porkkla-Udd, reinstate Russia actually, although not formally, in her pre-1917 positions on the Baltic and Arctic coasts; and Russian magnanimity towards Poland is rewarded by valuable gains in East Prussia, Bukovina and the Carpathians. The total area acquired by Russia between 1945 and 1947 is approximately as large as the total area lost between

1917 and 1921. Russia has redeemed the hostages she gave to defeat, revolution and national self-determination."

"The western frontiers of the Soviet Sphere of Influence coincide so closely with those Czarist Russia planned to draw after the defeat of the Central Powers that Czarist and Soviet policies appear to differ as regards methods only. From inter-Allied agreements concluded during World War I and the published statements of leading public figures, notably Russian and Czech, emerges the Czarist Government's Grand Design for eastern Europe: the frontier of Russian Poland was to have been pushed westward towards Stettin, bringing within the Russian Empire the Polish provinces of Germany and Austria; the north-eastern provinces of Hungary were to be ceded to Russia and a Greater Serbia and Greater Rumania were to receive additional territories carved from Hungary, leaving the latter country a small state wedged between Serbia (Yugoslavia), Rumania and a Kingdom of the Czechs ruled by a Russian Prince; and Russia was to receive the European possessions of Turkey inclusive of the Straits. The aggregate of annexed territories, protectorates, alliances and Pan-Slav affiliations would have extended Russian influence to the Oder River, the Alps, the Adriatic and the Aegean. The Czarist project, cleansed of the dynastic and social pre-conceptions of Czardom, took shape in the system of annexed territories, occupation zones, friendly regimes and ideological affiliations which constitutes the Soviet sphere of influence in Europe. It is only at the Straits that the Soviet Government failed to attain the goals set by its predecessors."

This explains, as Mr. X's analysis does not, the pattern and plan, not merely the generalized fact, of Soviet expansion, and also the causes and the issues of the diplomatic conflict in the postwar period—1945-1947.

The westward expansion of the Russian frontier and of the Russian sphere of influence, though always a Russian aim, was accomplished when, as, and because the Red Army defeated the German army and advanced to the center of Europe. It was the mighty power of the Red Army, not the ideology of Karl

Marx, which enabled the Russian government to expand its frontiers. It is the pressure of that army far beyond the new frontiers which makes the will of the Kremlin irresistible within the Russian sphere of influence. It is the threat that the Red Army may advance still farther west—into Italy, into western Germany, into Scandinavia—that gives the Kremlin and the native communist parties of western Europe an abnormal and intolerable influence in the affairs of the European continent.

Therefore, the immediate and the decisive problem of our relations with the Soviet Union is whether, when, on what conditions the Red Army can be prevailed upon to evacuate Europe.

7.

I AM contending that the American diplomatic effort should be concentrated on the problem created by the armistice—which is on how the continent of Europe can be evacuated by the three non-European armies which are now inside Europe. This is the problem which will have to be solved if the independence of the European nations is to be restored. Without that there is no possibility of a tolerable peace. But if these armies withdraw, there will be a very different balance of power in the world than there is today, and one which cannot easily be upset. For the nations of Europe, separately and in groups, perhaps even in unity, will then, and then only, cease to be the stakes and the pawns of the Russian-American conflict.

The material cause and reason of the conflict will have been dealt with.

The terms of the problem were defined at Yalta in the winter of 1945. There, with a victory over Germany in sight, Roosevelt, Churchill, and Stalin made a military settlement which fixed the boundaries where the converging armies were to meet, and were to wait while the governments negotiated the terms of peace which would provide for the withdrawal of the armies. The crucial issue in the world today is whether the Yalta military boundary, which was intended to be provisional for the period of the armistice, is to become the political boundary of two hostile coalitions.

The Yalta line registered an agreed estimate by Roosevelt, Churchill, and Stalin as to what would be the actual military situation at the close of hostilities. They knew that the Red Army would be in Warsaw, Bucharest, Budapest, Belgrade and Sofia. So Churchill and Roosevelt recognized that the military boundary for the armistice would place eastern Europe within the Soviet sphere. The British, on the other hand, were in Athens; the British-Americans were in Italy: therefore, Stalin recognized that Italy and Greece would be within the British and American sphere. The Americans, it was evident, were paramount in the Pacific and would play the leading part in the defeat of Japan. So the United States was recognized as the paramount power in Japan. There was some doubt as to where the Red Army and the western armies would meet in Germany and Austria. The Yalta line was, therefore, the result of a combined military estimate of where they would probably find themselves when the German resistance had finally been crushed. Actually the Americans advanced beyond that line. But at Yalta it was by no means certain that they would reach that line, and there is excellent authority for saying that Mr. Churchill felt he had made as good a bargain as British-American military prospects warranted.

The Yalta line in the Far East was settled on the same basis—that is to say, on an agreed estimate of the balance of power at the close of hostilities. There has been, I believe, a misunderstanding about this in the United States. The concessions made to Stalin by Roosevelt and Churchill have been represented as being the price they paid for Soviet intervention in the Japanese war. The concessions, it is then said, were unnecessary. For Japan was already defeated or would soon have been, what with the blockade, the air raids and the atomic bomb, and therefore no price need have been paid for Soviet participation.

Now it may be true, probably it is true, that Roosevelt and the American military command overestimated the strength of Japan, and that in agreeing to the Soviet claims they thought they were paying a price that had to be paid if the Japanese war was to be won completely and fairly soon. But, in fact, the Russians were in a position to occupy the territory they asked for and more besides, whether or not they entered the war. Their armies were on the borders of Manchuria and northern China, and ours were not. The concessions which Roosevelt and Churchill made to Stalin in the Far East were less than the Soviet Union had the power to take by its own force. Nothing was in fact conceded to Stalin that Roosevelt and Churchill could, if they had been put to the test, have been able to withhold.

The Yalta military boundary was the datum line from which the diplomatic settlement of the war had necessarily to begin. It was, I believe, at this juncture that American diplomacy became confused, lost sight of the primary and essential objective, and became entangled in all manner of secondary issues and disputes in the Russian borderlands.

The British and the Americans, of course, could not accept the permanent division of the European continent along the Yalta line. They could not accept a settlement in which Poland, Czechoslovakia, Yugoslavia, Hungary, Rumania and Bulgaria would lose all independence and become incorporated as Soviet republics in the U.S.S.R. They had a debt of honor to the countless patriots in those lands. They realized that if the frontiers of the Soviet system were extended as far west as the middle of Germany and Austria, then not only Germany and Austria but all western Europe might fall within the Russian sphere of influence and be dominated by the Soviet Union.

Thus for the best of reasons and with the best of motives they came to the conclusion that they must wage a diplomatic campaign to prevent Russia from expanding her sphere, to prevent her from consolidating it, and to compel her to contract it. But they failed to see clearly that until the Red Army evacuated eastern Europe and withdrew to the frontiers of the Soviet Union, none of these objectives could be achieved.

Had they seen clearly the significance of the military situation, they would not have committed the United States to anything in eastern Europe while the Soviet government had the power to oppose it, while the United States had no power to enforce it. They would have taken and noted the pledges and promises to respect the independence and the freedom of the nations of eastern Europe which Stalin gave them at Yalta. But they would not have committed the United States to a guarantee that Stalin would keep his pledges while his army was occupying eastern Europe.

For since the United States could not make good this guarantee, the onus of the violation of the pledges was divided between the Russians, who broke them, and the Americans, who had promised to enforce them and did not. It would have been far better to base our policy on the realities of the balance of power; to let Stalin, who made the promises which he alone could fulfill, take the whole responsibility for breaking them; to concentrate our effort on treaties of peace which would end the occupation of Europe.

For if, and only if, we can bring about the withdrawal of the Red Army from the Yalta line to the new frontier of the Soviet Union—and simultaneously, of course, the withdrawal of the British and American armies from continental Europe —can a balance of power be established which can then be maintained. For after the withdrawal, an attempt to return would be an invasion—an open, unmistakable act of military aggression. Against such an aggression, the power of the United States to strike the vital centers of Russia by air and by amphibious assault would stand as the opposing and deterrent force. And until treaties are agreed to which bring about the withdrawal of the Red Army, the power of the United States to strike these vital centers would be built up for the express purpose of giving weight to our policy of ending the military occupation of Europe.

All the other pressures of the Soviet Union at the "constantly shifting geographical and political points," which Mr. X is so concerned about—in the Middle East and in Asia—are, I contend, secondary and subsidiary to the fact that its armed forces are in the heart of Europe. It is to the Red Army in Europe, therefore, and not to ideologies, elections, forms of government, to socialism, to communism, to free enterprise, that a correctly conceived and soundly planned policy should be directed.

8.

WE MAY now examine a question which must be answered before the policy, which I contend is preferable to the Truman Doctrine, can be accepted with conviction. What about the communist parties which are also the instruments of Soviet power? If the Red Army withdrew behind the frontiers of the Soviet Union, the communist parties would remain—to put it bluntly, as a Soviet fifth column. They will be assisted, we may take it, by Soviet agents and by Soviet funds and Soviet contraband weapons and by Soviet propaganda and by Soviet diplomacy.

That is true. There will still be the problem of communism. Nevertheless, the heart of our problem is, I contend, the presence of the Red Army in Europe. The communist party in any country is the *fifth column*. It is, however, only a fifth column. There are the *other four columns*, and they are the Red Army. The policy which I suggest is designed to separate the first four columns from the fifth, to divide the Red Army from the Red International. For the Soviet power is most formidable where they are able to work together, that is to say, where the communist party has the support and protection of the Red Army.

There are, as I write, no communist states except within the zone of Russian military occupation. Outside the military

boundary of the Soviet orbit those countries are most threatened with a communist seizure of power into which the Red
Army could most easily march. Within the Soviet zone it
would be interesting to see what would happen if the occupying forces inside those countries or surrounding them were
withdrawn. For it is one thing to resist a local dictatorship and
quite another to resist the strongest land power on earth.

It is conceivable, though it has not yet happened, that a
communist party might win an election, or that it might seize
the authority of government though there was no Red Army
to support it and protect it. But even if this happened, the
position of the communist party would be incomparably less
secure than if the Red Army were present to overawe the
police and to suppress the resistance of the national army and
of the national forces. In an unoccupied country the communist fifth column would have to fight and win a civil war
before its authority was established. In an occupied country
the Red Army can prevent a civil war and drive the resistance
underground and reduce it to a guerilla action.

I do not think there is any doubt, therefore, that the evacuation of Europe by the Red Army would alter the situation
decisively. There would then be in the internal affairs of the
European countries no alien and irresistible military force
actually deciding or threatening to decide the internal issues
of power and authority.

The next question is whether the objective of obtaining the
withdrawal of the Red Army is attainable. A certain answer
to this question is, of course, impossible. We can only cal-
culate the probabilities, and we can say that the objective I am
contending for is concrete, substantial, intelligible to everyone, and a normal and universally accepted objective at the
conclusion and settlement of a war.

We may begin, moreover, by noting that in all our disagreements with the Soviet government the Kremlin has always agreed that the purpose of these tedious negotiations is in the end to conclude treaties of peace with all the enemy states. Now a treaty of peace may call for the annexation of territory, it may call for a period of supervision and control until the enemy state has fulfilled certain demands and has met certain conditions. But if it is a treaty of peace, it must provide for an end to military occupation. The treaties which have been signed with Italy and with the satellite states are definite on this point. If and when treaties of peace are agreed to for Germany and Austria, they will have to contain definite stipulations for the withdrawal of the armies of occupation. In some form or other, at some time or other, no matter what supervision and control are imposed upon, what guarantees are exacted from, Germany, and exchanged among the Allies, these treaties of peace will fix a time when the Red Army, and of course the British, the French and the American armies also, can no longer, as a matter of legal right, remain in central and eastern Europe.

Therefore, in making the withdrawal of the armies the objective of our policy, we are seeking to accomplish a result which the Soviet government by the very act of negotiating peace treaties has agreed to in principle.

This is something on which to work. For in our disagreements, which are deep and stubborn, there is a common commitment which no one has challenged. If there is agreement on the terms of the German and Austrian treaties, the withdrawal of the armies will follow. This is a wholly different kind of commitment from those which were made at Yalta and at Potsdam, and were then violated later. As to what is democracy and what is a free election and the like, it is possible to differ honestly and to differ dishonestly.

But an agreement to evacuate an army must either be carried out or violated. It is not a question for the dialecticians, the ideologists, the sophists and the casuists. It is not a matter which can be hidden behind an iron curtain. It is a matter of plain and quite obvious fact.

Now it may be that the Soviet Union, though committed in principle, will not in fact agree to a settlement which means the evacuation of Europe. If her purpose is the domination of Europe and of a large part of the world, she will never agree. For the military evacuation of continental Europe would not be one of those "tactical maneuvers" against which, quite rightly, Mr. X tells us to be on guard.

It would be a strategic change in the balance of power. For once the Red Army had been withdrawn behind the frontiers of the Soviet Union, it could not re-enter Europe without commiting an obvious act of military aggression, which would precipitate a general war. The pressure of the Soviets upon Europe by propaganda and infiltration would continue, but that pressure would no longer be backed up by overwhelming military power throughout eastern Europe and by the threat of military intervention in western Europe. Though Tito's army, and perhaps the Polish army, assuming them to be satellites of Moscow, could exert considerable military pressure locally on the neighboring states, they are not capable of conquering and dominating Europe except as contingents of the Red Army.

If the Kremlin really means to dominate Europe, it will not withdraw its armies which are halfway across Europe. Standing on the Elbe line in the middle of Europe and Austria, and on the vulnerable frontier of Italy, the Kremlin is in a far better position to advance farther west than it can be if it withdraws and stands on its own frontiers. The withdrawal of the army is, therefore, the acid test of Soviet conduct and purpose, incomparably clearer, more definite, more practical than whether or not they observe the Yalta Declaration in countries liberated from the Nazis but still occupied by the Red Army. Verbal agreements like the Yalta Declaration and the Atlantic Charter can be made the subject of endless tactical maneuvering. For agreements of this kind do not change the balance of power. But the evacuation of a continent would change the balance of power.

The Kremlin will understand this, and we must expect it to exact the highest price it can obtain for what would be a deep reduction of its present power and influence in Europe, or, if it means to conquer Europe, to obstruct any settlement which meant that the Russian armies must evacuate Europe.

We shall in either case have clarified the real issue. Instead of seeking "to contain" the Soviet Union all over the Eurasian continent, we shall have the initiative and a definite and concrete objective; at the best we shall know the terms on which the main conflict can be settled; at the worst the Soviet Union will have shown its hand on an issue—the liberation of Europe from non-European armies—where there will be no doubt whatever that our cause is just, and that we are the champions of freedom, and that the great masses of the people of Europe will be with us because we stand for the very thing which only traitors can oppose.

We shall have written off the liabilities of the Truman Doctrine which must in practice mean inexorably an unending intervention in all the countries that are supposed to "contain" the Soviet Union. We shall be acting once more in the great American tradition which is to foster the independence of other countries, not to use other countries as the satellites of our own power, however beneficent, and as the instruments of our own policy, however well meant. Our aim will not be to organize an ideological crusade. It will not be to make Jeffersonian democrats out of the peasants of eastern

Europe, the tribal chieftains, the feudal lords, the pashas, and the warlords of the Middle East and Asia, but to settle the war and to restore the independence of the nations of Europe by removing the alien armies—all of them, our own included.

We shall have a diplomatic policy that it would be exceedingly difficult for the cleverest propagandist to misrepresent. For everyone can understand such a policy. Practically everyone will wish us to succeed in it. For alien armies are hateful, however well behaved, just because they represent an alien power and are, therefore, a perpetual reminder that the people on whom they are quartered are not masters of their own destiny.

Alien armies are, however, never well behaved: invariably they become corrupted. Thus we may count confidently upon a mounting popular support if we make it our mission to emancipate the ancient and proud continent of Europe from the military control of non-European powers. We shall be drawing upon the elemental and unifying passion of patriotism in Europe which, when it is aroused, is a much stronger passion than factionalism or any ideology.

9.

THE evacuation of Europe can be accomplished only if we can negotiate, sign, and ratify a treaty of peace for Germany and for Austria to which the Soviet government is a party. For the peace treaties about eastern Europe, which is between Germany and Russia, cannot become effective until there are German and Austrian treaties. The Red Army will remain in eastern Europe as long as it remains in Germany and in Austria.

We must turn then to the problem of Germany, and how that problem is defined if we adhere to the Truman Doctrine and how defined if we adopt the alternative policy for which I have been contending.

In its approach to the German problem, which is crucial in a world settlement, we come upon the most dangerous and destructive consequences of what Mr. X calls a policy of firm containment and what the world knows as the Truman Doctrine. Here, ever since Secretary Byrnes went to Stuttgart in 1946 and addressed the German nation, we have been preparing the ground for a gigantic diplomatic disaster.

For the policy of containment envisages the western zones of Germany as an essential part of the "unassailable barriers" which Mr. X tells us we should erect in the path of the Soviet Union. Thus the German nation must, if the policy is to be made to work, participate in the coalition of the containing nations. That it may be willing to participate, it has been deemed necessary to evoke the sentiment of German "unity," and to cultivate the national patriotism of the Germans even to the point where we have allowed the ideal of the unity of Germany to displace the ideal of the unity of Europe.

The underlying assumption, which is implicit though unavowed, has been that since Germany has lost the eastern provinces to the Russians and to a Russian satellite, Poland, German national feeling will naturally be directed against the Soviet Union. Historical experience and the logic of the situation indicate, I believe, that this is a profound miscalculation. For we are encouraging the Germans to want something—namely, national unity—which we cannot give them except by going to war with Russia. Germany cannot have unity, as all Germans must understand unity, except by recovering the lost provinces of eastern Germany. We would have to conquer Russia and Poland in order to restore the eastern provinces to Germany.

But Russia can return them to Germany whenever she decides that an alliance with Germany is a vital Russian interest. This can be done by performing another partition of Poland, an act which the men who signed the Molotov-Ribbentrop pact of 1939 could carry out if they deemed it expedient and necessary. Or if they deemed it inexpedient to partition Poland again, but necessary to enlarge the truncated Reich, they can offer the German nationalists compensation in western Europe and elsewhere for the lost provinces in the east. Just as they gave the Poles the German provinces as compensation for the territory east of the Curzon line, so they could offer Austria to the Germans, perhaps Alsace-Lorraine, perhaps Denmark, perhaps the Netherlands and the mouth of the Rhine.

We do not need to know exactly what the Soviet Union would offer the Germans for an alliance. It is enough to know that in an auction for the support of the Germans the Russians could offer them great prizes, and that we can offer the Germans absolutely nothing—except some help in rising from squalor and misery and prostration to the position of a fifth-rate power living a prosaic and stunted national existence. The idea that we can foster the sentiment of German unity, and make a truncated Germany economically strong, can keep her disarmed, and can use her in the anti-Soviet coalition is like trying to square the circle. Applied to Germany, the policy of containment is a booby trap, constructed by men who do not understand the politics of power.

The controlling fact in the German problem is that by the advance of the Red Army beyond Berlin and because of the annexations which resulted from it, the Soviet Union has destroyed the unity of the Reich and has acquired the power to restore the unity of the Reich. The western nations cannot restore the unity of Germany, and it is therefore suicidal for them to incite the sentiments of unity, and to treat the western portion of Germany as a prospective ally in the operation of the Truman Doctrine. For if Germany is to become allied on either side of the diplomatic conflict, the precedents of history and the logic of the situation tell us that when she is strong enough to be a useful ally to anyone, she will become the ally of Russia. The more we bring what remains of Germany, after the dismemberment of the east, under the unified control of a German government, the more profitable and the easier it will be for Berlin and Moscow to make a deal and become allied. If Hitler and Stalin, Ribbentrop and Molotov could make a deal, how can we dare to suppose that a Germany ruled by communists, socialists and nationalists would not make a deal?

And if we carried the policy to its ultimate end, as Mr. Hoover has asked us to do, and made a separate treaty of peace with western Germany, we should have made a German-Russian alliance even more certain. The German government with which we had made peace would again be a sovereign power: it would have to have at a very minimum the sovereign right of an independent state to have diplomatic agents abroad and to receive them, and to use the diplomatic apparatus of codes, couriers, and agents.

Having made a separate treaty of peace with us, the new central German government would necessarily have to begin negotiations for separate treaties of peace with its eastern neighbors—with Poland, Czechoslovakia and with Russia. She would enter these negotiations, having gotten from us all that she could expect—which would not be much and not nearly enough to satisfy a German patriot. The negotiations with the east would offer the great prizes and all manner of temptation. These negotiations would take place with the Red Army in eastern Europe and in what had been the eastern provinces of Germany, and as a matter of fact with the Red Army in Berlin. Thus Russia, which alone can offer the German nationalists great inducements, would also be in a military position to compel the German nationalists to enter into a deal.

Once we recognized the consequences of the fact that Germany had been dismembered in her eastern provinces, it would become plain that we could not use western Germany to contain Russia. It would become plain, too, that the unity of Germany could not be restored by the United States. Therefore there can be no German settlement, which is tolerable, by re-establishing the sovereign power of a central German government in a truncated area and dedicated to the unity of Germany. The annexations in the east of Germany demand a radical decentralization of western Germany.

The truncated area will have to be decentralized, not unified, and the German states which are in it will have to take their places within a larger European system and a European economy. Not German unity but European unity, not German self-sufficiency but European self-sufficiency, not a Germany to contain Russia but a Germany neutralized as between Russia and the west, not the Truman Doctrine but the Marshall Plan, purged of the Truman Doctrine, should be the aims of our German policy.

These will be sound aims even if we find it impossible to agree with the Russians on a treaty of peace. For we shall have identified ourselves with a policy which opposes the revival of the German power to threaten her neighbors, not with a policy which would place them in a German-Russian nutcracker, would compel them to choose sides for a Third World War, and would make their territory the battlefield of that world war and of the enormous civil war which it would surely precipitate.

Though we could not conclude an agreement with the Russians, we should be identified with a policy which, if an agreement could be concluded, would mean the evacuation of the continent, and the restoration of Europe to the Europeans. Thus, as the diplomatic struggle continued, we should stand forth ever more clearly as the champions of the vital interest of all the peoples of Europe.

We could then leave it to the Europeans to decide how much they are willing to have paid in reparations, in concessions and trade agreements, and as ransom, in order to get the Russians to withdraw the Red Army. If we were wise, and were more interested in settling the war than in making gestures of our disapproval of the Russians and of communism, we should offer to contribute our part to the ransom—if paying ransom will achieve the main objective.

If, nevertheless, the Soviet government will not negotiate an agreement, if the price of a settlement is impossibly high, if the ransom is deliberately set in terms which mean that Russia does not intend to evacuate Europe, the situation will be no more dangerous than it is today. But our energies will be concentrated, not dispersed all over the globe, and the real issues will be much clearer.

10.

IN THE introduction to this essay, I said that Mr. X's article on "The Sources of Soviet Conduct" was "a document of primary importance on the sources of American foreign policy" in that it disclosed to the world the estimates, the calculations, and the conclusions on which is based *that part* of American foreign policy which is known as the Truman Doctrine. Fortunately, it seems to me, the Truman Doctrine does not have a monopoly. Though it is a powerful contender for the control of our foreign policy, there are at least two serious competitors in the field. One we may call the Marshall line, and the other is the American commitment to support the United Nations.

The contest between the Truman Doctrine on the one hand, the Marshall line and the support of U. N. on the other is the central drama within the State Department, within the Administration, within the government as a whole. The outcome is still undecided.

The real issue is hidden because the Truman Doctrine was promulgated shortly after General Marshall became Secretary of State, and because he made the decision to go to the support of Greece and Turkey, which was a concrete application of the Truman Doctrine. The issue is confused by the fact that Mr. Molotov and the Soviet propaganda abroad and many publicists here at home are representing the Marshall proposals to Europe as an application of the Truman Doctrine. The confusion is compounded still more because the Director of Secretary Marshall's Planning Staff is now known, through the publication of Mr. X's article, to have been the leading expert upon whose observations, predictions, and hypotheses the Truman Doctrine is based.

Nevertheless, if we look at the two main theaters of American diplomatic interest—at China and at Europe—and if we fix our attention on Secretary Marshall's approach, we can see a line of policy developing which is altogether different from the line of the Truman Doctrine. General Marshall's report on China, which has now been reviewed and confirmed by General Wedemeyer, made it quite clear that in his judgment we could not, and should not, attempt the kind of intervention in China which we are carrying on in Greece. The Marshall and Wedemeyer reports do not argue that we can contain the Soviet Union and erect unassailable barriers in its path by participating in the Chinese civil war, as we are in the Greek civil war, and by underwriting Chiang Kai-shek's government as we are underwriting the Athens government. The Marshall line in China is not an application of the Truman Doctrine, but of an older American doctrine that we must not become entangled all over the world in disputes that we alone cannot settle.

Yet the Marshall line in China is not isolationist. It would not end in our ceasing to interest ourselves in China and in giving Russia a free hand. But it is emphatically not the line of the Truman Doctrine which would involve us as partisans in the Chinese conflict and as patrons of one faction.

The line of the Marshall policy in China is to disentangle the United States, to reduce, not to extend, our commitments in Asia, to give up the attempt to control events which we do not have the power, the influence, the means, and the knowledge to control.

The proposal which Secretary Marshall addressed to Europe in his Harvard speech last June was animated by the same fundamental conception—as China's problem has to be dealt with primarily by the Chinese, so European problems have to be dealt with primarily by Europeans. Thus there was no "Marshall Plan" for Europe: the essence of his proposal was that only a European plan for Europe could save Europe, or provide a basis on which the American people could prudently and fairly be asked to help Europe save itself. The Marshall proposal was not, as Mr. Molotov and many Americans who do not understand it have tried to make out, an extension to Europe as a whole of the experiment in Greece. Quite the contrary. In Greece we made an American plan, appropriated the money, entered Greece and are now trying to induce the Greek government to carry out our plan. In the Harvard speech Secretary Marshall reversed this procedure. He told the European governments to plan their own rehabilitation, and that then he would go to Congress for funds, and that then the European governments would have to carry out their plans as best they could with the funds he could persuade Congress to appropriate.

The difference is fundamental. The Truman Doctrine treats those who are supposed to benefit by it as dependencies of the United States, as instruments of the American policy for "containing" Russia. The Marshall speech at Harvard treats the European governments as independent powers, whom we must help but cannot presume to govern, or to use as instruments of an American policy.

The Harvard speech was delivered about three months after President Truman's message. Much had happened in those three months, and all of it had gone to show that while Con-

gress and the people were willing to applaud the Truman
Doctrine, because they are exasperated with Russia, they were
not going to support it with the funds and blanket authority
which it requires. Though the President got the funds he asked
for in order to apply his doctrine in Greece and Turkey, he
got them after a long delay and in circumstances which were
tantamount to telling him not to come back too soon for much
more. The plans which existed for extending the Truman
Doctrine to Korea and then to a series of impoverished, dis-
ordered and threatened countries on the perimeter of the
Soviet Union were discreetly shelved.

Yet a crisis, enormously greater than that in Greece or
Korea or Iran or Turkey, was developing. It was a crisis of the
British Empire, and of France, and of Italy, and indeed of the
whole western world. Extraordinary measures of American
assistance were obviously going to be needed. After Congress
had showed its attitude last spring, there was no possibility
that this assistance would be provided by applying the prin-
ciples, the procedure, and the precedent of the Truman Doctrine, as it had been revealed in the Greek affair. A wholly
different conception and a radically different approach were
necessary if the crisis of the western world was to be dealt with.

Out of the knowledge that the Truman Doctrine was unworkable in Europe, that Congress would not support it
anyway, and that a constructive revival of European collabo-
ration was imperatively necessary, the policy of the Harvard
speech was conceived. And I think it is true to say that those
who conceived it were concerned not only to devise a way by
which Europe could be saved from economic disaster, but also
to devise a graceful way of saving the United States from the
destructive and exhausting entanglements of the Truman
Doctrine.

They may not succeed. If the planning of policy in the Truman Administration were to be dominated by the conclusions propounded by Mr. X, the Marshall proposals would fail. For the European crisis is insoluble if Europe remains divided by the iron curtain, raised by the Russians, and by the containing wall which we are supposed to construct.

But there are reasons for thinking that the Russians will not be able to maintain the iron curtain and that we cannot construct western Europe as a containing wall. They are that the vital needs of the people of Europe will prevail: the economic interdependence of western and eastern Europe will compel the nations of the continent to exchange their goods across the military, political and ideological boundary lines which now separate them.

The great virtue of the Marshall proposal is that it has set in motion studies abroad and in this country which will demonstrate conclusively that the division of Europe cannot be perpetuated. And since the division of Europe came about because the Red Army and the Anglo-American armies met in the middle of Europe, the withdrawal of these armies is necessary if Europe is to be reunited. The Harvard speech calls, therefore, for a policy of settlement, addressed to the military evacuation of the continent, not for a policy of containment which would freeze the non-European armies in the heart of Europe.

The Marshall studies will show that the industrialized areas of western Europe cannot be supported, except to relieve their most pressing immediate needs, from North and South America. They must revive their trade with the agricultural regions of eastern Europe and with European Russia. If they do not do that, the cost of maintaining a tolerable standard of life in western Europe will be exorbitant, and the effort to meet it will require a revolutionary readjustment of the economic life of the whole Western Hemisphere.

At the same time studies made in Warsaw, Prague and in Moscow will show that the problems of eastern Europe are insoluble without increasing economic intercourse with western Europe. Thus from all quarters in eastern Europe and in western Europe, in Washington and in Moscow, the pressure will increase to reunite the divided economy of Europe —and perhaps to go on towards a greater unity than ever existed before.

11.

WE MAY now consider how we are to relate our role in the United Nations to our policy in the conflict with Russia. Mr. X does not deal with this question. But the State Department, in its attempt to operate under the Truman Doctrine, has shown where that doctrine would take us. It would take us to the destruction of the U. N.

The Charter and the organization of the United Nations are designed to maintain peace *after* a settlement of the Second World War has been arrived at. Until there is a settlement of that war, the United Nations does not come of age: it is growing up, it is at school, it is learning and practicing, it is testing its procedure, gaining experience. During this period, which will not come to an end until the great powers have agreed on peace treaties, the United Nations cannot deal with disputes that involve the balance of power in the world. The balance of power has to be redressed and settled in the peace treaties by the great powers themselves, principally, as I have tried to show, by the withdrawal of their armies from the continent of Europe.

Until such a settlement is reached, the United Nations has to be protected by its supporters from the strains, the burdens, the discredit, of having to deal with issues that it is not designed to deal with.

The true friends of the United Nations will, therefore, be opposed to entangling the world organization in the Soviet-American conflict. No good and nothing but harm can come of using the Security Council and the Assembly as an arena of the great dispute, or of acting as if we did not realize the inherent limitations of the Charter and thought that somehow we could by main force and awkwardness use the United Nations organization to overawe and compel the Russians. All that can come of that is to discredit the United Nations on issues that it cannot settle and thus to foreclose the future of the U. N., which can begin only if and when these issues have been settled.

Judging by the speeches in the Greek affair of the British and the American delegates, Sir Alexander Cadogan and Mr. Herschel Johnson appear to be acting on instructions which treat the U. N. as expendable in our conflict with Russia. It is a great pity. Nothing is being accomplished to win the conflict, to assuage it, or to settle it. But the U. N., which should be preserved as the last best hope of mankind that the conflict can be settled and a peace achieved, is being chewed up. The seed corn is being devoured.

Why? Because the policy of containment, as Mr. X has exposed it to the world, does not have as its objective a settlement of the conflict with Russia. It is therefore implicit in the policy that the U. N. has no future as a universal society, and that either the U. N. will be cast aside like the League of Nations, or it will be transformed into an anti-Soviet coalition. In either event the U. N. will have been destroyed.

12.

AT THE root of Mr. X's philosophy about Russian-American relations and underlying all the ideas of the Truman Doctrine there is a disbelief in the possibility of a settlement of the issues raised by this war. Having observed, I believe quite correctly, that we cannot expect "to enjoy political intimacy with the Soviet regime," and that we must "regard the Soviet Union as a rival, not a partner in the political arena," and that "there can be no appeal to common purposes," Mr. X has reached the conclusion that all we can do is to "contain" Russia until Russia changes, ceases to be our rival, and becomes our partner.

The conclusion is, it seems to me, quite unwarranted. The history of diplomacy is the history of relations among rival powers, which did not enjoy political intimacy, and did not respond to appeals to common purposes. Nevertheless, there have been settlements. Some of them did not last very long. Some of them did. For a diplomat to think that rival and unfriendly powers cannot be brought to a settlement is to forget what diplomacy is about. There would be little for diplomats to do if the world consisted of partners, enjoying political intimacy, and responding to common appeals.

The method by which diplomacy deals with a world where there are rival powers is to organize a balance of power which deprives the rivals, however lacking in intimacy and however unresponsive to common appeals, of a good prospect of successful aggression. That is what a diplomat means by the settlement of a conflict among rival powers. He does not mean that they will cease to be rivals. He does not mean that they will all be converted to thinking and wanting the same things. He means that, whatever they think, whatever they want, whatever their ideological purposes, the balance of power is such that they cannot afford to commit aggression.

In our conflict with Russia a policy of settlement—as I have sought to show—would aim to redress the balance of power, which is abnormal and dangerous, because the Red Army has met the British and American armies in the heart of Europe. The division between east and west is at that military boundary line. The meeting of those armies caused the division. No state in eastern Europe can be independent of the Kremlin as long as the Red Army is within it and all around it. No state in western Europe is independent while it is in effect in the rear of this military frontier. The presence of these non-European armies in the continent of Europe perpetuates the division of Europe. The Soviet government has been communist for thirty years. For more than a hundred years all Russian governments have sought to expand over eastern Europe. But only since the Red Army reached the Elbe River have the rulers of Russia been able to realize the ambitions of the Russian Empire and the ideological purposes of communism.

A genuine policy would, therefore, have as its paramount objective a settlement which brought about the evacuation of Europe. That is the settlement which will settle the issue which has arisen out of the war. The communists will continue to be communists. The Russians will continue to be Russians. But if the Red Army is in Russia, and not on the

Elbe, the power of the Russian communists and the power of the Russian imperialists to realize their ambitions will have been reduced decisively.

Until a settlement which results in withdrawal is reached, the Red Army at the center of Europe will control eastern Europe and will threaten western Europe. In these circumstances American power must be available, not to "contain" the Russians at scattered points, but to hold the whole Russian military machine in check, and to exert a mounting pressure in support of a diplomatic policy which has as its concrete objective a settlement that means withdrawal.

Then we shall know what we are trying to do. The Russians will know it. Europe will know it. We shall be trying to do a great thing which is simple and necessary: to settle the main actual consequences of this particular war, to put an end to the abnormal situation where Europe, one of the chief centers of civilization, though liberated from the Nazis, is still occupied by its non-European liberators.

We shall be addressing ourselves to an objective to which our own power is suited—be it in diplomacy or in war. We shall be seeking an end that all men can understand, and one which expresses faithfully our oldest and best tradition—to be the friend and the champion of nations seeking independence and an end to the rule of alien powers.